The Gift Year
Blessings, Grace, and Wings!

Kimberly Ann Borin, Ed.D.

Copyright © 2018 Kimberly Ann Borin. All rights reserved. No part of this book may be used or reproduced by graphic, electronic, or mechanical means, including photocopying, recording, videotaping, or by an information storage retrieval system, without the written permission of the author, except in the case of brief quotations embodied in critical articles and reviews.

Because of the dynamic nature of the Internet, any Web addresses or links in this book may have changed since publication and no longer be valid.

The Gift Year, front and back cover design by
Kimberly Ann Borin, Copyright © 2017.
The Gift Year illustrations and photographs by
Kimberly Ann Borin, Copyright © 2015, 2016, 2017.
Front Cover Art, *Angel Party Girl*, by
Kimberly Ann Borin, Copyright © 2017.
Back Cover Art, *Waves of Mercy and Grace*, by
Kimberly Ann Borin, Copyright © 2017.
Photograph on back cover of Kimberly Borin, by
Melanie Smith, Copyright © 2017.

Formatting: Judy Loose, www.looselinks.com
Editing: Tracy Ivie, www.wordsandideas.net
Published by: Kimberly Ann Borin, Ed.D.

ISBN-13: 978-0-692-92102-9
ISBN-10: 0-692-92102-8

Library of Congress Control Number: 2017917044
Kimberly Ann Borin Ed.D., Lebanon, NJ

Dedication

This book is for my friends, who inspire me to create and breathe life into something new.

Acknowledgements

I continually feel blessed to know many loving and kind people in the world. I would like to thank my family, those near and far, who are always encouraging and supportive. My friends, who walk with me on the trail, listen to my ideas, cheer me on, offer just the right amount of encouragement, at just the right time. As they make changes in their life and travel in new directions, they inspire me to do the same. My neighbors are also a tremendous gift to me. They look out for me and are always there to lend a hand, to listen to a story, or to share one of their own.

This year, many people helped me learn to listen in a new way. Father Bill at the Loyola House worked with me to pursue a 10-month study of the 19th Annotation. We met weekly and explored the spirit's leading and I was fortunate enough to learn about Ignatian Spirituality with him as an exceptional teacher.

The Shalem Institute also continually offered lessons in contemplative living as I pored through past readings, copious notes, and artwork I had created on retreats. Along the way, I felt privileged to be with a spiritual director's support group, to be in spiritual direction, and to offer direction to others as well.

Listening within a community of love and support is a tremendous affirmation of faith. The Church of the Holy Spirit also offers that affirmation of care and believing in hopes and dreams. I feel fortunate to spend time with people from the Church of the Holy Spirit and to be amidst so many creative and compassionate people.

The College of Saint Elizabeth, a place where I teach and take classes, is also a tremendous resource. They offer students a chance to live into their goals and careers, all while supporting them in an inclusive and sacred space.

I am grateful for all of my friends who are teachers, counselors, and life coaches in and outside of a school setting. They always bring a spirit of optimism and energy. Their positive outlook on life continues outside of the classroom as they lift everyone around them with a sense of possibility.

My friends who are artists are also such an inspiration. So many people create, cook, design, imagine, write, and bring beauty wherever they go. They remind me that there is much more to do, explore, and express. They also offer me the courage to express in ways that are unique to my own journey. This requires tremendous daring as the feelings of vulnerability in expressing and sharing new work is daunting. I also want to thank Judy Loose and Tracy Ivie who help me breathe life into new books. It is never an easy process. I am so grateful for their expertise, kindness, and patience.

I would also like to acknowledge the charming portals and places I have been. Throughout the year, I would find myself in new places that were slightly hidden, lovely, and deeply peaceful. These gardens, libraries, mansions, labyrinths, museums, and hospital waiting rooms became places of wonder. These were magical places that offered silence, time away from the busy places, and a sense that things were just as they should be. In those places everything seemed just right. Along the way, I also met new people who seemed like old friends and wise souls.

Lastly, I would like to thank the daring ones. These are the people I know (and maybe sometimes have never met) who are willing to question, to get out of the race in progress, and who believe that dreaming in a new way is good and essential. I admire all of the people I know who are artists, entrepreneurs, athletes, and more who were willing to try something new and were rewarded in ways they had not imagined. Thank you for your courage and for lighting the way.

Thank you to you, the reader. I hope that perhaps just one small piece of this book offers a glimpse of your own gift year. May it be the start of a new journey filled with blessings for you and those you love. Thank you.

Table of Contents

Introduction *1*

The Gift Year *13*

   Offer Yourself a Gift Year *14*

   Take a Chance on Intentions *16*

   Celebrate the Process of Getting There *18*

   Create a New Slogan *20*

   Pray with a Community of Saints *22*

   Notice All of the Invitations *24*

   Listen for Discernment and Action *26*

   Return Home a Safer Way *28*

   Surrender *30*

   Find Charming Portals *32*

   Trust the Unfolding and the Buffet Approach *34*

   Learn Something New *36*

   Teach Something New *38*

Blessings *41*

   Make Friends with Liminal Space *42*

   Trust in Transformative Movement *44*

   Deepen Compassion for Yourself and Others *46*

   Love Your Rebellious Self *48*

   Celebrate All of Your "Impossible" Victories *50*

Grieve and Forgive *52*

Tell Your Story *54*

Pray and Paint Your Process *56*

Celebrate Your Courage *58*

Do Something Small *60*

Design Your Own Process for Healing *62*

Hear the Whisper of Your Heart *64*

Notice What You Need Minute by Minute *66*

Grace *69*

Choose Nourishing and Wholeness *70*

Blossom! *72*

Decorate with Words *74*

Notice All of the Surprising Gifts *76*

Give Thanks *78*

Reflect on Your Journey *80*

Make Goody Bags *82*

Trust that All Appointments are Divine *84*

Ask the Difficult Questions *86*

Walk with Sophia *88*

Pay Attention to Dreams *90*

Design Your Own Beautiful Structure *92*

Pray in New Ways *94*

Wings! *97*

Rest *98*

Find Light *100*
Make a Promise to Yourself *102*
Create New Recipes *104*
Embrace Change as You Can *106*
Sit by the Sea *108*
Spread Your Wings! *110*
Listen for Your Prophet's Call *112*
Celebrate Your Success *114*
See Grace Everywhere *116*
Leave the Race in Progress *118*
Shelter in Place *120*
Strengthen Your Foundation *122*

Books for the Journey *125*
About the Author *129*
Books by Kimberly Ann Borin *131*

Introduction

The Gift Year
It was the time of summer solstice and a night of the full moon, known as the rare Strawberry Moon. I decided to offer myself something called *the gift year*. During the prior year, I had been wondering what I needed and thought about how many high school graduates are now taking a "gap year."

"That is just what I need," I thought to myself. Then, I thought, "No, I need a *gift year*." In that moment, the idea was born. The phrase struck me immediately with its sense of hope, playfulness, and relief! It gave me a sense of where I needed to go. I began to write and draft out what I thought this idea of the gift year was all about.

I decided that it included a year of simplicity, learning to follow my heart, and knowing how to take better care of myself. I resolved that, along the way, I would record with a grateful heart what I was learning through art, photographs, writing, and maybe even cooking! I decided to also take a leap of faith to attend seminary and pursue an internship as a chaplain.

My goal and hope was to restore my sense of peace and to heal my spirit and heart. Perhaps I had seen too much and perhaps I had been trying too hard to control everything around me. I felt exhausted and weary, wondering how to return to a sense of calm, safety, and joy. I wanted the freedom and responsibility to live into something new and to try to understand this beautiful idea from God of the gift year.

I hoped that from my own daring, in creating artwork and in moving in a new direction that I might also encourage others to breathe life into more of who they are and who they are meant to be. It is with this sense of adventure and daring that I began, but in a very small and timid way.

Blessings

As I started to sort out what I intended for this gift year, I wrote lists of ideas, words, and tasks ahead. I made notes on scraps of watercolor paper, torn-out journal pages, the edges of magazine articles, and whatever was around at the time. I labeled a folder *"The Gift Year"* and tossed in all the scraps of paper and some of the intentions I hoped to live into. I didn't know if I could sustain myself or live into any of the ideas, but I dared to take a chance anyway. My list of intentions and eventual blessings included:

Live a simple life.
Clean out, make more space.
Write a seventh book.
Take the time to breathe life into my own business, learn about marketing, and expand it to someday make a living from it.
Create and deliver at least one inspiring talk.
Teach more yoga.
Take two walks a day.
Do more of what I love.
Capture all of the gifts and record what I am learning through writing, watercolors, art, and photography.
Spend more time in nature.
Restore my sense of playfulness and safety.
Let go of control.
Conserve and protect my energy.
Spend more time laughing with children.
Learn about beauty.
Learn to make delicious risotto.

Arriving at this new year, and being willing to take a risk was not as easy as I thought it would be. I had already pursued more than a year in spiritual direction and was praying with a group of spiritual directors, to be able to come to this place of knowing what I wanted to do. I knew that nothing was impossible in God's eyes and I had to trust that what I was being led to do was right.

Even though I had the support of many people and had thought about a gift year for a long time, it was beyond frightening. I was not prepared for the onslaught of angst that arrived when I decided to take the leap into this special year. I experienced first an enormous sense of relief and then a barrage of emotions like fear, turmoil, shame, worry, despair, and serious doubt. I argued with myself, I put myself down, I thought that perhaps I was not capable of anything else and maybe had been a complete failure all along.

I did not realize how difficult it would be and I did not anticipate the number of tears I would shed before, during, and even after the year. Despite this, I knew it was what I needed to do. I had to follow this very small whisper and ache within my heart. If I didn't, I knew that I would never be able to help others do the same. So, I decided to leave my job to pursue my dream of going to seminary.

During this time, I rested, dried my tears, walked with friends, talked with people who were retired, and just tried to navigate all of the feelings I had. It was surprising that they all existed at the exact same time. I experienced courage and fear, joy and grief, excitement and despair, all with lots of breathing in between.

Along the way, I met new people, felt a gentleness in my spirit, and allowed myself to take time with people. I was able to offer kindness and attention that I had not offered before. I found myself worried, but less irritated, and so happy to have time to write, draw, paint, photograph, explore, and walk. I was also happy to take the time to read, to unstack the dishwasher, to gently fold my clothes, to clean out, and to write a letter without having to multitask. This new sense of gentleness, awareness, and expansiveness felt like luxury. I appreciated every small moment of freedom that I was granted.

This appreciation allowed me to return to a feeling of deep gratitude for everything around me and for what I had been given. The people I met, the walks I took, the flowers I noticed, the raindrops I heard, and the time for resting felt like a gift. I was beyond grateful and tried to say *thank you* to whoever was listening, as often as I could.

One of the blessings I also experienced was learning how to create a new focus. Being a public relations major, I knew that a new slogan or ad campaign or mantra would help keep me focused and guide me into something new. As I began, I was constantly slowing down and reminding myself to just breathe. I tried to breathe one moment at a time and to trust that everything about this new year would be revealed in its own divine time.

As I did this, I was reminded of the power of breath, something I am very familiar with as an athlete and yoga teacher. For me, this simple act of breathing took on a new meaning. I was learning to breathe in more of life (literally) and trust that the sense of peace I received would sustain me on my new journey.

I decided that *Breathe In Life* would be my new slogan for my year and my business. It would be a reminder that with a simple breath, we can all learn something new, deepen our spirituality, and listen to the small voice of our hearts.

Previously, during the final retreat for the Shalem Institute when I began to think about this new year of adventure, I also decided to create my own hero team, a community of saints to inspire me and help breathe in new life. These were people who also knew the power of slowing down, daring, standing up, and walking in a way that connected with a heart's call. My list included:

Mary, The Blessed Virgin, Cesar Chavez of California,
Stephen Biko of South Africa, Nelson Mandela,
Archbishop Desmond Tutu,
Sir Gawain the Green Knight, Jesus,
The Archangels Michael, Gabriel, Raphael and Uriel,
Thich Nhat Hanh, Dorothy Day of New York, Mother Teresa,
Mohandas Gandhi of India, St. Francis of Assisi,
St. Clare of Assisi,
Reverend Dr. Martin Luther King, Jr., Writers, Poets,
Artisans, Julia Child,
My Parents, My Grandparents,
and Jane Addams.

Grace

As I learned to slow down, I received not only blessings, but also moments that felt like pure grace. I also received many invitations to do things I had not done before. Something about the gift year gave me permission to say "yes" to lots of new things, things I wouldn't have considered in the past. I soon became aware of all of the invitations that were presented to me that I had not noticed, or had the courage to respond to before.

These invitations included giving talks, teaching yoga in new ways, learning to paint, interning as a chaplain, going back to school, learning about the *Ignatian Spiritual Exercises*, and deepening the roots of my own faith. I was able to edit a biography, read to children, learn about preschool, and even try new marketing strategies.

Along the way, I gave a talk and offered *Ten Simple Ways to Enhance Your Spirit*, things that I was also learning at the time. You will see some of these themes listed here and throughout the book, they include:

*1. Celebrate all of your victories
(the large, the small, the impossible!).
2. Create a community of saints to cheer you on.
3. Take all of the time that you need to discern and choose.
Take one beautiful moment at a time.
4. Try on different ideas and throw out the ones that don't
work for you.
5. If the next step seems too big, take a smaller,
more reasonable step.
6. Grieve, cry, let go, and offer yourself permission
to begin again.
7. Nap, rest, rest, and rest some more to find your own center. Breathe deeply and slowly, as often as you can.
8. Create your own recipe for nourishing your mind, body,
and spirit.
9. Love your rebellious self, use your voice,
and tell your story.
10. Trust that your tender, gentle, healing heart
is a reflection of God and greater love.
Trust that you are loved.*

I was aware that these new invitations were also a "call" to learn something new, explore happiness, and expand my horizons. I wanted to grant myself permission to answer the question, "What invitations for joy call to you today?"

The practice of yoga also offered me new ways to learn and moments of grace. I realized that all of the movements in yoga could also help me spiritually and deepen my sense of peace. I decided to stretch my ability to wait for just the right thing, reach for something new in the waiting, breathe along the way, stand tall and confident, and be open for what was next. I learned to bend toward things that seemed life-giving and filled with light. I promised myself that I would learn to be present to what "is" within and without, and embrace my own fear, breathing in courage along the way.

In addition to yoga offering moments of grace, I also learned to listen for discernment as I went through the 19th Annotation, where I met weekly with Father Bill. I wanted to listen for what I was being called to do. The 19th Annotation is a spiritually guided program of the *Ignatian Spiritual Exercises*, helping people discern with God, their next most sacred step. The exercises are offered by a Jesuit priest and spiritual director and are done daily within a thirty-day period, or over a longer period of time, as I had done.

I learned that we can trust that we will be able to do what we are called to do in the world, even what might seem like an impossible task. I also learned that claiming something as your own and traveling in a new way is not for the faint of heart. Many people who love you will have an opinion about what you should or should not do, all with heartfelt intentions. In the end, it will be between you and your heart and listening to your sense of God or Spirit.

This year of listening also taught me about surrender and letting go. I liked to think that I was very good at that, but the truth was that I wanted to control everything – and maybe even offer some judgment along the way. One night, I even had a dream about learning to let go and surrender.

The dream revealed an action and thought process that looked like a watercolor with salt – and stars. In the letting go of whatever it was, a light in the form of bright aqua stars and beauty emerged. This could happen only when you had done all that you could do and offered the rest of it up (literally upwards) and released it.

In the dream, it was clear that letting go, surrendering to God, Spirit, Love, Mercy, or the Universe allowed for beauty and light to be revealed in ways that effort could not create. Seeing this image and receiving the understanding of the beauty of letting go offered me a feeling of peace and relief. In learning to surrender, I also learned how to be present, nourish myself, and blossom in a new way.

Wings!

In addition to blessings and grace, wings showed up in the most unexpected of ways. One day during the winter, I became interested in learning how to create an angel wing! I did not realize that this simple act of exploring an angel wing would offer me the encouragement of angels that embrace all of us as we grow in new ways.

To create the wing, I started with tissue paper to learn how wings are constructed. I cut out feather shapes in a variety of bright colors and collaged them on a square piece of cardboard. Then, I tried drawing and painting with watercolors. I painted black grackle wings, pastel butterfly wings, and what I thought might be angel wings too.

I was eager to try my hand at painting on canvas but very nervous about knowing what to do. I had painted on canvas once, twenty years ago, during a small class at the YMCA. I summoned up my courage, found a 50% off coupon for Michael's ™, where I discovered the perfect small canvas. As I made my way to the cash register, something about the project didn't feel right. Perhaps, I had misread my eagerness to paint; perhaps my ideas were too big for what I was capable of doing.

Then, I realized that what I wanted to express was too big, but not because I couldn't do it – because the canvas was too small! I returned to the painting aisle and pulled down a four-foot by three-foot canvas. I stood there looking at it with awe and, yet, something about it felt just right.

The girl at the register asked me if I was a professional painter. When I said, no, I was just starting out; she was surprised that I chose to work on such a large canvas. It gave me pause for reflection, but I was undaunted.

When I got home, I took out my old paintbrushes from the garage and began experimenting with my new kit of acrylics. I quickly realized that the large canvas would require much more paint, specialized brushes, and maybe even some instruction.

On the advice of a friend, I began to experiment with gel paints, flexible paste, metallic paints, paper clay, and glitter too! As I began working with the wings, I was aware of the many gifts of learning and the blessings that were emerging. While I painted, I felt a deep sense of peace as I saw how encouraging, hopeful, and loving angels and their wings could be.

I learned how to use new tools, materials, and mediums. I also learned how my yoga practice of movement, breath, strength, and stretching helped for painting on large surfaces. Painting renewed my courage to take a leap of faith and offer myself a fresh start. The light, color, inspiration, and beauty that continually emerged also felt like moments of grace.

As I wrote this book, I was preparing for an art show called *Angels Waiting in the Wings*. I was surprised that at the culmination of my journey of discernment and the gift year, I was having an art show to share four-foot tall angel wings!

A few nights before the show, I went through my journals and folders of notes and drawings to see what I had learned during the year. I saw that on August 12, 2016, I had painted a simple butterfly, with the words, *Breathe in Life, Spread Your Wings*!

That date was exactly one year to the day of the *Angels Waiting in the Wings* art show. I know that the wings were for me and perhaps for others too. I continue to be surprised by the gifts of blessing and grace offered by the Spirit and how angels and their wings show up in the most unexpected of ways.

Gifts of the Journey

Taking the gift year allowed me to create and celebrate a process of growing into something new. Noticing the blessings, gifts, and invitations helped me to see new opportunities for growth and possibility. These moments also revealed a sense of peace and grace that helped me to understand self-care for mind, body, and spirit. On another level, these moments offered me the chance to surrender and let things go as I was able.

The wings that were revealed also offered me the encouragement of moving forward on the journey – no matter what that meant. I felt embraced by wings, perhaps from the angels I painted, or the people I prayed with, or the moments of silence and breathing.

With all of these gifts, I was granted a constant feeling of gratitude. I was so appreciative of every small thing that was revealed, every moment of peace, each moment of rest, and all of the people along the way. I still feel that sense of gratitude for each new moment of possibility that I receive and the chance I have to breathe life into something new.

I also realized that there is so much more to say and do! I realized that I still have so much more to learn, as all beginners do. Again, I was struck by the privilege of being able to learn and grow in new ways, to understand more about a variety of faiths, and to be present. I also learned that I want to continue to do more of what I love and that perhaps this is part of my calling. There were many other lessons I learned and that I continue to learn.

For You

In this little book, my hope is to share a selection of the lessons I learned and the art I created throughout the year. I have also included art from previous years as well. I hope that a few of the words or the pictures speak to you and offer you the light and hope you need for your own gift year. I hope that a word of courage, or care, or hope brightens your own next step as you breathe life into something new.

At the end of the book, I have provided a list of books that offer information, encouragement, and stories about discernment for the journey of life. Perhaps these books will offer just what you need for your journey. Along the way, I wish you every good thing as you continue to follow the whisper of your heart.

The Gift Year

Offer Yourself a Gift Year

Take a quiet moment to see what it is that you need. Listen to your heart and see what is calling to you. It may sound like a very small whisper. Note what you hear, and claim it. Offer yourself time in a gift day, or maybe even a few gift minutes. Take the time that you need to offer yourself permission to live with a bit of adventure as you breathe life into something new.
Listen, trust, and follow the whisper of your heart.

Take a Chance on Intentions

As you live into your moments of a new adventure, see what intentions are revealed for you. What would you like to happen? What is calling to you? What would bring your heart joy? What would allow you to travel lightly in the world? What are your gifts?
How will the world be blessed by your presence and your gifts?
Take a chance on new intentions today.

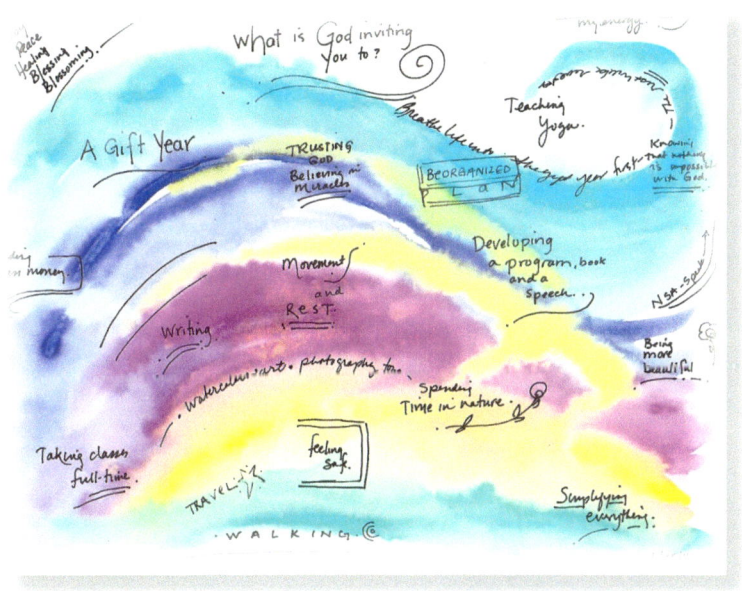

Celebrate the Process of Getting There

Deciding to do something new is not easy. We often arrive at that place because of suffering, pain, worry, sadness, or fear. Celebrate your courage for making it through the difficulties and arriving at the place of the next most beautiful decision.
Trust that each new, small step will be revealed to you at just the right time.
Celebrate the process of arriving where you are.

Create a New Slogan

Take a moment to imagine that you are an advertising executive. Look at all of the slogans, logos, and ads that motivate you. Create a new slogan for yourself and your new adventure. Don't feel that you have to find the perfect slogan, just one that feels right for today. Then, if another idea arrives, create another new slogan.
Trust that the words will shape your new adventure.

Pray with a Community of Saints

Trust that you are not alone. Call upon all of the inspiring people, spirits, and saints who remind you of who you are and who you are meant to be. Trust that new people will also arrive who are eager to celebrate you and all that you are daring. Allow yourself be loved and cared for by the people around you.
Pray and play with a community of saints.

Notice All of the Invitations

What invitations for joy are calling to you today? Grant yourself permission to learn something new, explore happiness, and travel in a new direction, or maybe several. Say "yes" to unexpected invitations and trust that you will learn a great deal about yourself as you breathe life into something new.
Let your tender heart say "yes."

Listen for Discernment and Action

As you go forward, continue to discern what feels right for you. Perhaps the answer comes from your heart, your head, your gut, a friend, or a group of trusted people. Take the time to discern what feels right. Sometimes action provides the discernment we need too. Trust that discerning the next step is an ongoing process of listening and taking small action steps.
Be present to your heart and spirit.

Return Home a Safer Way

In discerning your journey, you may feel that you need to protect your new ideas and your unfolding path. Create healthy boundaries and limits on your time, energy, health, and spiritual life. Claim safety and protection as your own. If necessary, go home by a different and safer way.

Surrender

Do all that you can. When you have done it all and can do nothing else, rest, sit down, and surrender. Trust that things are unfolding behind the scenes and that letting go is an essential part of the process. Know that sometimes the freedom you gain in surrendering is valuable to
everyone around you too.
Give yourself permission to surrender to something larger.

Find Charming Portals

Look for magical, enchanted, charming portals. These may be new places, cottages, libraries, museums, local parks, or maybe just a playground. Notice places that sparkle like gems with just a hint of joy and comfort! You'll know when you find them because you will sense a lovely bit of playfulness and peace. These charming portals will also enhance and affirm your new adventure.
Enjoy!

Trust the Unfolding
and the Buffet Approach

Trust that your own gift year is important and unfolding. Even if you don't make any physical changes in your life, just the act of choosing to learn something new will shape your time and your journey. Trust the unfolding of your life, one small moment at a time. Choose the buffet approach, just notice, walk slowly, sample items before you, and don't make any large decisions. Trust that joy is continually unfolding for you.

Learn Something New

Take a chance to learn something new. Allow yourself to be in that awkward, uncomfortable place where you are reminded of your younger student self. Trust that learning and the courage to learn matters. Your willingness to step into something new will also inspire those around you. Trust that there is so much more that you are capable of learning and doing.
Take a chance to learn something new.

Teach Something New

As you learn something new, you will begin to teach something new, too. So often as we learn, students arrive who may be in need of what we are learning. As we teach, we can continue to practice what we are learning.

Believe that what you have to teach and share will empower others. Know that what you share is often the blessing that those around you may need. Trust that what you know is good enough to teach, right now.

Blessings

Make Friends with Liminal Space

*When you take on a new adventure, you will inevitably end up in liminal space. This is a disconcerting place of not being where you were, and not being where you are going.
Congratulate yourself for your willingness to walk with mystery and victory in
this uncomfortable and new place.
Be present to each moment and be gentle with yourself.
Create and move forward with tenderness, as you are able.*

Trust in Transformative Movement

As you move into a liminal and new space, trust that small movements will help sustain and transform you. Transformation also comes from shifting your body in simple ways. Practice good posture, walking mindfully, breathing deeply, and stretching in new ways.
Move in new ways with new shoes, new paintbrushes, new stirring spoons, and new dance steps.
Trust that these movements will help you to transform, heal, and blossom.

Deepen Compassion for Yourself and Others

*Treat yourself in a precious way. Offer yourself tender compassion and then, you can easily offer it to others. Promise yourself that your body, mind, and spirit are too precious to be broken down by outside influences or too much stress. Offer yourself the beauty, wholeness, and nourishment you need.
Trust that you are beautiful and worthy.*

Love Your Rebellious Self

Love your rebellious self. Extend the compassion you have for yourself to all that you have done or not done. Trust that all of your decisions were right at the time. Trust your gut and all that you have learned along the way. Love your amazing, courageous, rebellious self.
If saying that out loud brings a smile to your face, say it again tomorrow!

Live into Restorative Possibility

Be · Breathe · Restore · Blossom

8/2/14

Celebrate All of Your "Impossible" Victories

Take a moment to remember all of things that you have done. Take a moment to remember all of the things that you have accomplished that you once thought were "impossible." Notice and celebrate all of your victories, the big ones and small ones too! Notice what victories currently feel impossible and trust that they will work out too. Think about how you will celebrate them in the future and do what you can in the meantime.

Grieve and Forgive

Some journeys forward bring the feelings of loss and grief for what we have left behind. Grant yourself permission to grieve, cry, weep, or just lie on the couch and be sad. Be present to the sadness and let the tears come to help you let go. Give yourself permission to grieve, so you can heal and offer the same courage to others. If you can forgive along the way, that will be healing to you as well. Trust that grieving and forgiving is a process that may take a long time.

Tell Your Story

Tell the story of your journey.
Take the time to express where you have been
and where you are going. Talk about the good
times, the tough times, the times where you had
no idea what you were doing.
Tell it in writing, painting, baking, quilting,
acting or more.
Share your story, and trust that it matters
to everyone who hears it.

Pray and Paint Your Process

*Take time to pray and maybe even paint your process. Often we focus on just the end result of our journey. Sometimes, the magic and all we are learning is happening right now, in the moment, in the process of the journey. Try to give words, feelings, color, and shape to all you are learning. Play with new mediums that give way to water, air, movement, and color and show up differently than you expected.
The revelations that come with creativity and art will help you understand your own process.*

I thought to myself, "I must paint today - no matter what!"

Perhaps, it is the hope of colors running together or the movement of the brush or maybe even the coolness of the water. We shall see...

8/12/14

Celebrate Your Courage

Celebrate your courage and willingness to take one small step – even if you are not sure what is next. Congratulate yourself for being willing to travel through the unexpected, the yucky, and sometimes dangerous, all while protecting your beautiful heart, spirit, and gift.

Do Something Small

When starting your journey, just do something small to begin. Laugh, eat raisins, put on your socks, and add an easy task to your list. Take one very small, simple step forward and trust that the next step will be revealed when you are ready.
Do something small.

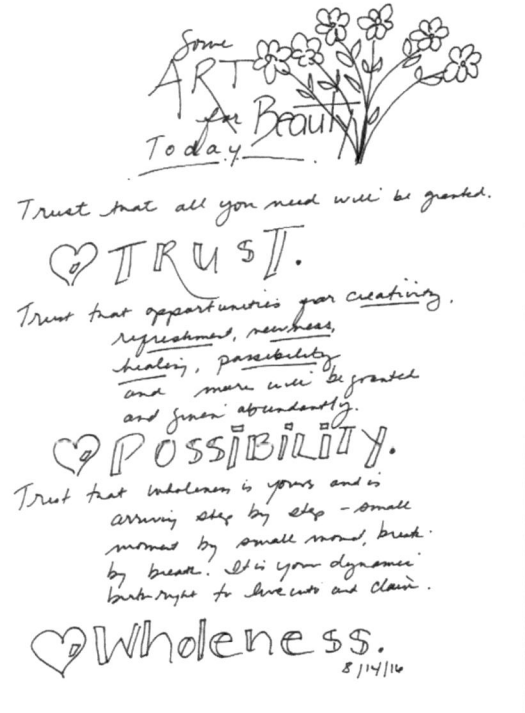

Some ART for Beauty Today.

Trust that all you need will be granted.

♡ TRUST.

Trust that opportunities for creating, refreshment, newness, healing, possibility and more will be granted and given abundantly.

♡ POSSIBILITY.

Trust that wholeness is yours and is arriving step by step — small moment by small moment, breath by breath. It is your dynamic birthright to live into and claim.

♡ Wholeness.

8/14/16

Design Your Own Process for Healing

Everyone heals in a different way. Choose your own process for healing. Perhaps it involves making smoothies, or crocheting, or walking the Appalachian Trail, or even dancing.
Trust that your particular process for healing is just what you need.
Design your own amazing process for healing into wholeness.
Trust that it will inspire others to do the same.

Beautiful xxx
Child of God....

Today.
Notice Moments of Joy. Playfulness,
Creativity. Love and Hope for the Future.
Each Moment
is a chance to see something new,
to breathe, to be open to prayer, to
notice Grace.

3/14/17

Hear the Whisper of Your Heart

Be still. Listen and trust the small, barely noticeable whisper of your heart. Notice what you are being invited to do. Listen to the resistance but listen to the larger "yes" too. Take a leap of faith to move in the direction of "yes."
Trust that the whisper of your heart matters.

Serve.
Stretch.
Notice
 Gifts.
Go to the
 Beach.
Believe that
all of the
 simple
  moments
   matter. 8/2/16

Notice What You Need Minute by Minute

As you listen to your heart, you will hear what it is that you need. Perhaps you are thirsty, or tired, or the old shoulder injury is bothering you. Perhaps you will want to play, or celebrate, or throw a party.
Attend to what it is that you need each moment.

Grace

Choose Nourishing and Wholeness

Choose the most nourishing thing, each time you have a choice. Breathe in grace, seek refreshment, take action, affirm your presence, and walk with courage to nourish your spirit. Allow yourself to be embraced and know that you are loved along the way as you give birth to something new.

Give yourself permission to choose nourishing and to choose wholeness.

Blossom!

*Trust in your beautiful process of blossoming.
Trust that each step is allowing you to grow and blossom in a new and fuller way.
Celebrate your gifts, strengths, and dreams, too.
Offer yourself the courage to share your gifts and dreams. Trust that when you do, you will encourage other people to blossom into their full potential.*

Decorate with Words

Find words that nourish you. Post them around your living space, think about what they mean to you, and live into them. Here are a few to start: Breath, Movement, Mindfulness, Awareness, Inspiration, Blessing, Heart's Desire, The Spirit's Invitation, Nature, Story, Voice, Creativity, Vision, Healing, Presence, Rest, Angels, Elegance, Beauty, Surrender, Grace, and Grounding.

Notice All of the Surprising Gifts

Along the way, you will be given gifts that might often take you by surprise. Perhaps you'll receive a challenging learning opportunity, a chance to hold someone's hand, a job that you didn't think you could do, or the opportunity to develop your strengths.
Trust that everything is a gift.
Trust that the surprising gifts are also moments of love.

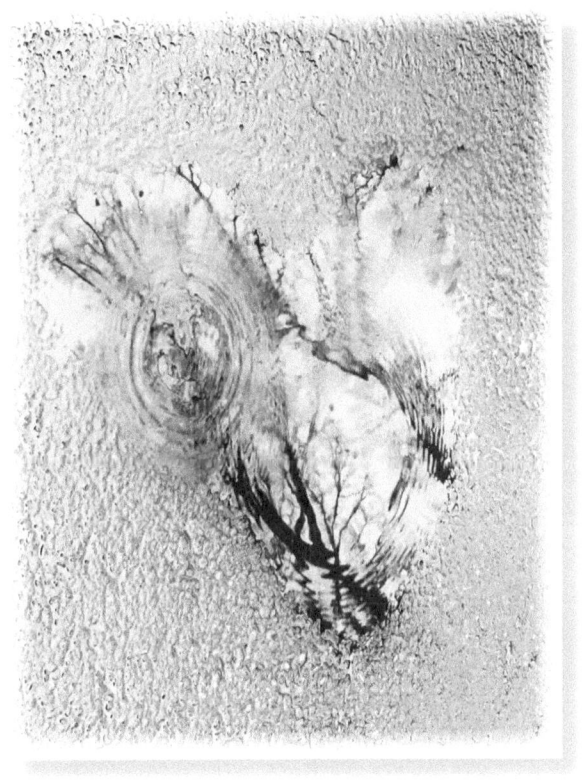

Give Thanks

Take a moment to give thanks for each new breath, each new day, and all you have at the moment. Give thanks, if you can, even for the difficult times. Trust that new learning and miracles are on their way to you, sometimes behind the scenes. Take the time to notice how energizing a simple Thank You can be.

Reflect on Your Journey

As you travel, take time to reflect upon where you have been and where you are going. Notice all of the small victories along the way and what you have learned. Take time to share this with someone else, as your reflection will help others on their journeys too. Keep track of your reflections, as this will help you know how are you growing.

Make Goody Bags

Goody bags are often given out at children's birthday parties. There is something purely delightful and playful about giving and receiving them. Make a goody bag for yourself with small items that remind you that you deserve the gift of celebration and joy!

Trust that All Appointments are Divine

Trust that each moment has its own inherent gift. You may wonder: What am I doing here? What is the purpose of this meeting? Trust that the appointment you have been given is meant for you, and take time to see the blessing within. Know that you bring healing to others, no matter where you are.

Ask the Difficult Questions

When you are taking time to be silent, lots of things will be revealed. Some insights will be pleasant, and others very unpleasant. Summon the courage to ask the difficult questions. Then, take time to offer yourself a gracious and compassionate response.

Trust that as you are asking the questions, good things are happening behind the scenes and that the answers will be revealed.

Walk with Sophia

As you walk forward in your journey, walk with wisdom, otherwise known as Sophia in the Greek language. Trust that the answers will come from within and you will know what to do next.

Trust in your own sense of wisdom and knowing, and have faith and courage as you walk with mystery.

Pay Attention to Dreams

Notice all the elements of your dreams if you can. See what they mean to you and if they offer a solution to a problem. Notice the people, landscapes, scenes, actions, colors, and feelings they bring.
Take time to see how the elements of your dreams speak to you and bring light to the next step of your journey.

Design Your Own Beautiful Structure

*You are the architect of your life. Only you can create a structure for each day that matters to you. Play around with different structures for the hour, the day, the workplace, or even a space to play.
Know that designing a new structure can take time, patience, trial and error.
Trust that you will design a beautiful structure that nourishes you on every level.*

Pray in New Ways

*Pray in a new way that makes sense to you.
Perhaps this means sitting in church, or holding
someone's hand, or baking a cake, or hiking on
a trail with reverence for the natural world.
Perhaps praying means sitting in silence, or
talking with God, or repeating the prayers you
love. Allow your moments of prayer to be filled
with an awareness of the Holy.
Take time to create and pray in new ways that
nourish and bless you.*

Wings!

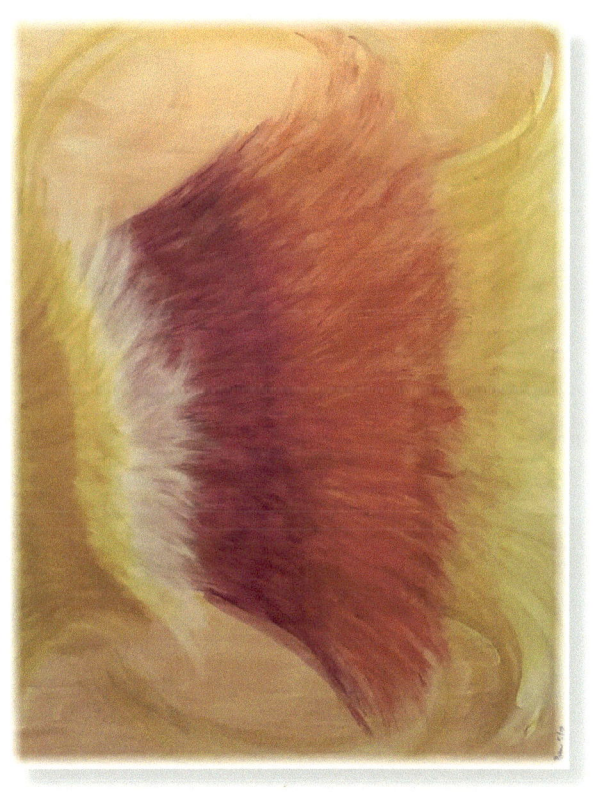

Rest

When you are trying to breathe life into something new, you may need more rest. Find moments of rest and reprieve, and allow yourself to sit awhile. It may be five minutes, thirty minutes, or a true Pajama Day. Trust that the rest is nourishing you and your dreams and will bring greater clarity and creativity.

Dear Little One,

Welcome to the world! You are a blessing and gift to the world. Welcome to your new days, a new journey and a new adventure. Each new and beautiful thing you encounter points the way. Trust that you are loved and embraced by grace. Take all of the time you need to dream big, be in nature, believe in miracles. Notice your angels along the way and have fun. Follow your beautiful heart and listen for the Spirit of Joy within.

Find Light

Find bits of light to remind you of hope and joy.
Notice the stars, glittery, sparkly stuff, candles,
lightning bugs, anything.
Trust in the light you bring to the world and the
light that guides you too.
Find the light within and around you and let it
inspire and lead you.

Make a Promise to Yourself

Make a promise that you will take good care of yourself. Abandon shame, forgive yourself, heal beautifully, and claim more for yourself. Offer yourself something more nourishing, more supportive, and more loving.
Celebrate You!

Create New Recipes

Create new recipes for your life. Think about the ingredients you need for joy, success, beauty, and true happiness.
Maybe your ingredients include laughter, time, friends, singing, or pesto pasta!
Visualize what you need and create a gorgeous recipe to bring it to life!

Embrace Change as You Can

Change is not easy, nor for the faint of heart. Be gentle with yourself as you learn to go with the flow of change. Trust that you are held and are safe along the way.
Give yourself permission to resist change and to move forward when you are ready.
Embrace change and healing as you can.
Offer yourself all of the time that you need.

Sit by the Sea

Take the time you need to be in nature. Sit by the sea, walk in the woods, throw stones in the pond, search for worms, or watch the clouds.
Offer yourself moments in nature that heal you, that remind you of how precious you are, and that nourish your growing spirit.
Delight in wonder, awe, and curiosity.
Remember what it was like to be a child in the outdoors. Breathe in some fresh air and take time to play.

Spread Your Wings!

Every bird has to fledge and you do too! Try something new, sing out loud, make art, and wear outrageous clothes. Offer yourself a chance to spread your wings, and see all that you can be. You can choose to do something barely noticeable, something small, or something bold.

Give yourself a chance to spread your wings and take one small step today.

Listen for Your Prophet's Call

Take time to listen for your prophet's call. It might seem like an invitation to do something beyond what you imagined.

You might think you aren't good enough, ready enough, or smart enough, but trust that the call is meant for you.

Trust your ability to walk into a new adventure and know that you have what it takes.

Celebrate Your Success

After you have taken a big step or completed something from your list of tasks, celebrate. Take a moment to acknowledge what you have done; savor the success and rest before moving forward.
Trust that each celebration offers a little bit of momentum for the journey ahead.

See Grace Everywhere

Try to notice bits of grace everywhere. Perhaps you'll hear a child laughing, or maybe a chocolate cupcake will show up, or you'll watch birds flying elegantly in the sky.
Heighten your awareness for the gifts of grace that show up.
Allow these gifts to inspire you and nourish your spirit.
Trust that grace is happening all around you every moment.

Leave the Race in Progress

You are allowed to leave the race that is in progress at any time.
As you see other people racing around, you may feel that this is essential for living.
Not true.
You are allowed to leave the race at any time, and trust in your own peaceful journey.

Shelter in Place

We often hear about people sheltering in place before a storm.
Sheltering in place means to be grounded, to remain in a simple place, to be safe, to be nourished, to be sustained. Sometimes this is necessary for our everyday life as well.
Do what you need to shelter in place to feel safe and protected.

Strengthen Your Foundation

To feel grounded, we often need to strengthen our foundation.
This means, simplify your life, clean out your closet, pay your bills, weed the garden, or just live in a sustainable way. Sometimes this means, purifying your diet, doing sit-ups, breathing deeply, or maybe
wearing good shoes.
Do what you must do to strengthen your foundation, as it is the best way to begin again.

Books for the Journey

Addison, Howard *A. Show Me Your Way, The Complete Guide to Exploring Interfaith Spiritual Direction.* Woodstock, VT: Skylight Paths Publishing, 2014.

Benner, David G. *Presence and Encounter, The Sacramental Possibilities of Everyday Life.* Grand Rapids, MI: Brazos Press, 2014.

Borgeault. Cynthia. *The Wisdom Way of Knowing.* San Francisco, CA: John Wiley & Sons, Inc., 2003.

Chittister, Joan. *Called to Question, A Spiritual Memoir.* Lanham, MD: Sheed & Ward, 2004.

Chodron, Pema. *The Places That Scare You, A Guide to Fearlessness in Difficult Times.* Boston, MA: Shambhala Publications, Inc., 2001.

Coles, Robert. *The Spiritual Life of Children.* Boston, MA: Houghton Mifflin Company, 1990.

Dougherty, Rose Mary. *Discernment, A Path to Spiritual Awakening.* New York: Paulist Press, 2009.

Epperly, Bruce G. and Solomon, Lewis D. *Mending Our World, Spiritual Hope for Ourselves and Our Planet.* Philadelphia, PA: Innisfree Press, Inc., 2002.

Fiorenza, Elisabeth Schussler. *Jesus, Miriam's Child, Sophia's Prophet.* New York, NY: The Continuum Publishing Company, 1995.

Freire, Paulo. *Pedagogy of the Oppressed.* New York, NY: The Continuum International Publishing Group, Inc., 2001.

Hanh, Thich Nhat. *Mindful Movements, Ten Exercises for Well-Being.* Berkeley, CA: Parallax Press, 2008.

Hanh, Thich Nhat. *The Energy of Prayer, How to Deepen Your Spiritual Practice.* Berkeley, CA: Parallax Press, 2006.

Hirshfield, Jane. *Women in Praise of the Sacred, 43 Centuries of Spiritual Poetry by Women.* New York, NY: Harper-Collins Publishers, Inc., 1994.

Johnson, Elizabeth. *She Who Is, The Mystery of God in Feminist Theological Discourse.* New York: The Crossroad Publishing Company, 2000.

Johnson, Elizabeth. *Truly Our Sister: A Theology of Mary in the Communion of Saints.* New York, NY: The Continuum International Publishing Group, Inc., 2009.

Labowitz, Shoni. *God, Sex and Women of the Bible, Discovering Our Sensual, Spiritual Selves.* New York, NY: Simon & Schuster, 1998.

Labowitz, Shoni. *Miraculous Living, A Guided Journey in Kabbalah through the Ten Gates of the Tree of Life.* New York, NY: Simon & Schuster, 1996.

Ladinsky, Daniel. *Love Poems from God, Twelve Sacred Voices from the East and West.* New York, NY: The Penguin Group, 2002.

Linn, Dennis., Linn, Sheila. F., Linn, Matthew. *Sleeping with Bread, Holding What Gives You Life.* Mahwah, NJ: Paulist Press, 1995.

Loori, John Daido. *The Zen of Creativity, Cultivating Your Artistic Life.* New York, NY: Ballantine Books, 2005.

O'Donohue, John. Beauty: *The Invisible Embrace, Rediscovering the True Sources of Compassion, Serenity, and Hope.* New York: HarperCollins, 2004.

Pinkola Estes, Clarissa. *Untie the Strong Woman*. Boulder, CO: Sounds True, Inc., 2013.

Savary, Louis M. *The New Spiritual Exercises, In the Spirit of Pierre Teilhard de Chardin*. Mahwah, NJ: Paulist Press, 2010.

Silf, Margaret. *Inner Compass, An Invitation to Ignatian Spirituality*. Chicago, IL: Loyola Press, 1999.

Tutu, Desmond. and Tutu, Mpho. *Made For Goodness and Why This Makes All the Difference*. New York, NY: HarperCollins Publishers, 2010.

About the Author

Dr. Kimberly Ann Borin is an author, artist, yoga teacher, and spiritual director. She believes that we can find joy and grace in simple moments. She has been a teacher and counselor since 1989 and holds a doctorate in education and master's degrees in both educational leadership and college counseling. She is also an Ananda Yoga teacher for adults and children and the author of the *Laughter Salad* and *Angel Pages* series of books. Her most recent book was *Gravy, Not Soup*. You can learn more about Kimberly at: www.TheEncouragingWorks.com.

Books by Kimberly Ann Borin

Laughter Salad, A Nourishing Mix of Inspiring Stories — In this collection of inspirational true stories and playful art, Kimberly shares vignettes and times of synchronicity, serendipity, and miracles that bring us closer to our heart's desires—reminders that we are exactly where we need to be. Through the stories told, *Laughter Salad* reminds us that our journeys matter and that along the way we offer gifts to make the world a better, brighter place.

Laughter Salad for Little Ones, A Gentle Mix of Nourishing Letters for Children — Welcome to the world's most encouraging alphabet! This tender collection of words, affirmations, and letters will lift your spirits and help you remember that you are a gift to the whole world. The words are written for children, but they are intended to nourish everyone, whether you are a teacher, counselor, or parent. This book also contains *Seven Simple Moments*, which are meant to bring peace, inspiration, and relaxation wherever you are. Flipping through any page in *Laughter Salad for Little Ones* is sure to bring a bit of light, laughter, and celebration to your day!

Learning and Growing with Laughter Salad, A Mix of Nourishing Activities for Children Celebrating Nature, Relaxation, and Stories — This book offers more than 60 activities that bring simple moments of peace, relaxation, and nourishment to the lives of children and the adults who work with them. This is the perfect book for teachers, counselors, parents and anyone who works with children. The book is divided into three chapters that highlight lessons using nature, relaxation, and stories. In a matter of minutes, these activities can help students can feel more centered, calm, and connected to everything around them. These mindful moments also help children develop a deeper compassion for themselves and others.

Angel Pages, Words, Whimsy, and Art to Brighten Your Spirit and Heart — *Angel Pages* is a book of words and art to bring comfort to your spirit and heart. These simple and playful drawings created by Kimberly offer encouraging words to remind you that you are a gift to the world. Kimberly calls these pages *Angel Pages* because when she sits down to draw, she never knows what will show up. Just browsing through the pages, you may find a word, a drawing, or even a placement of color that inspires you to breathe life into your dreams and your journey, too!

Angel Pages for You, Journaling Space to Breathe Life Into Your Dreams — In this book, you'll find art, questions for reflection, and space to write, draw, and explore your hopes and dreams. Some of the themes for exploration include: miracles, beauty, taking your time, being brave, and living into possibility. This journal offers gentle encouragement to nourish you and to help you take small steps toward your most beautiful dreams.

Gravy, Not Soup and Other Moments of Grace — This is the perfect gift for the journey of life. These 52 stories of hope remind us of the grace that exists in our everyday moments. These gifts help us deepen our awareness of the inspiration and peace constantly being offered to us. These humble and funny recollections also give us the permission we need to move forward, knowing that everything is unfolding just as it should. *Gravy, Not Soup* serves up just the right nourishment for your life's journey.

www.ingramcontent.com/pod-product-compliance
Lightning Source LLC
Chambersburg PA
CBHW041622220426
43662CB00001B/19